VERTICAL MILLING
IN THE HOME WORKSHOP

FOR HOME MACHINISTS

VERTICAL MILLING
IN THE HOME WORKSHOP

FOR HOME MACHINISTS

Workshop Practice Series

ARNOLD THROP

Technical Reviewer,
Paul Fiege

FOX CHAPEL
PUBLISHING

© 1977, 1986, 1988, 1989, 1990, 1991, 1993, 1995, 1996, 1998, 2000, 2003, 2004, 2006, 2008, 2010, 2012, 2017, 2020, 2025 by Arnold Throp and Fox Chapel Publishing Company, Inc.

All rights reserved. *Vertical Milling in the Home Workshop for Home Machinists* is a revised edition of *Vertical Milling in the Home Workshop*, published in the UK in 2004 by Special Interest Model Books.

Technical Reviewer: Paul Fiege, CNC Machinist Faculty, Minneapolis Community and Technical College

ISBN 978-1-4971-0524-9

Library of Congress Control Number: 2025936540

To learn more about the other great books from Fox Chapel Publishing, or to find a retailer near you, call toll-free at 800-457-9112 or visit us at www.FoxChapelPublishing.com.

We are always looking for talented authors.
To submit an idea, please send a brief inquiry to acquisitions@foxchapelpublishing.com.
Or write to:
Fox Chapel Publishing
903 Square Street
Mount Joy, PA 17552

Printed in China

© Special Interest Model Books
An imprint of Fox Chapel Publishers International Ltd.
20-22 Wenlock Road
London
N1 7GU

www.foxchapelpublishing.co.uk

First published 2025
Text copyright 2025 Arnold Throp
Layout copyright 2025 Special Interest Model Books

ISBN 978-085242-843-6

Arnold Throp has asserted his right under the Copyright, Design and Patents Act 1988 to be identified as the author.

All rights reserved. No part of this publication may be reproduced in any form, by print, photography, photocopying, microfilm, electronic file, online or other means without written permission from the publisher.

Printed and bound in China

Because working with milling machines and other materials inherently includes the risk of injury and damage, this book cannot guarantee that creating the projects in this book is safe for everyone. For this reason, this book is sold without warranties or guarantees of any kind, expressed or implied, and the publisher and the author disclaim any liability for any injuries, losses, or damages caused in any way by the content of this book or the reader's use of the tools needed to complete the projects presented here. The publisher and the author urge all readers to thoroughly review each project and to understand the use of all tools before beginning any project.

Contents

PREFACE   11

Chapter One   **EVOLUTION OF THE VERTICAL MILL**   **12**
Early history of industrial machines: milling in the early small lathes: milling attachments for lathes circa 1920s: E.T. Westbury's experimental machine 1964: the Dore-Westbury machine 1968: currently available small machines and attachments.

Chapter Two   **MILLING FLAT SURFACES**   **27**
Surfaces parallel to table: simple fixed-radius flycutters: variable-radius boring head flycutting: multiple-tooth face mills: work holding: multiple-pass milling: surfaces square with table: using side of endmill.

Chapter Three   **SLITTING AND CUTTING**   **35**
Use of slitting saw for cutting through machinery component bosses: eccentric sheaves and straps: marine type big ends of connecting rods.

Chapter Four   **KEYWAY CUTTING**   **37**
Endmilling round ended 'feather' keyways: keyways on taper shafts: use of disc type cutters for plain sunken keyways: Woodruff keyways: making Woodruff cutters in the home workshop: table of suggested sizes of Woodruff keys and keyways for model engineers.

Chapter Five   **FLUTING COMPONENTS OTHER THAN TOOLS**   **43**
Correct form of flutes in loco connecting and coupling rods: mounting rods against angleplate for fluting: parallel flutes: taper flutes: preferred type of cutting tool.

Chapter Six **BORING** **45**
Dealing with parts too large to swing in lathe: boring large holes.

Chapter Seven **'JIG-BORING'** **46**
Using the mill as a measuring machine: drilling holes at one setting of work and precise centers: engine beam: back-lash precautions: trip gear component: multi-hole boiler plates.

Chapter Eight **PROFILING** **49**
Curves on parts too large for lathe: loco frames: smokebox castings: machine pad bolts: loco connecting rods and coupling rods.

Chapter Nine **END-ROUNDING** **52**
Use of hardened filing guides deprecated: mounting work on rotary table: standard size guide plugs: anti-slip precautions: direction of feed for external and internal surfaces.

Chapter Ten **DIVIDING HEADS** **54**
Simple ungeared dividing heads: using change wheels as index plates: examples of dividing work: hexagons, squares, dog clutch teeth: avoiding odd numbers: the Myford worm-geared dividing head: avoiding back-lash errors: packing block for bringing to lathe center height: universal steady stand for Myford head: three further dividing heads.

Chapter Eleven **DIVIDING HEADS AND GEAR-CUTTING** **62**
Limitations to straight spur gears: simple head: Myford worm-geared head: tooth cutting on integral pinion: use of home made flycutters: Brown & Sharpe disc type cutters: selection of cutter to suit number of teeth: cutting a large coarse tooth gear: anti-slip back-up devices.

Chapter Twelve **DIVIDING HEADS AND TOOL MAKING** **66**
Fluting taps: example 5-flute Acme tap: producing a small fine tooth milling cutter with ball end: use of table stop blocks: combination of rotary table with main table movement: large 60 degree countersink fluting.

| Chapter Thirteen | **DIVIDING HEADS AND GRADUATED SCALES** | **71** |

Cutting graduation marks: use of rotary 'engraving' cutters: use of non-rotating planing type tools: use of table stops to control line lengths: graduating cylindrical scales: graduating flat angular scales: checking correct way of figuring when stamping scales.

| Chapter Fourteen | **CUTTER SPEEDS FOR VERTICAL MILLS** | **74** |

Speeds affect time occupied on job: speeds too high may cause excessive cutter wear and chatter: rigidity of work, cutter and machine inferior as a rule to industrial conditions, dry cutting instead of lubricated: Table III gives speeds for cutters in different kinds of tasks: machine speeds may not always be suitable.

| Chapter Fifteen | **WORK-HOLDING WITH DIFFICULT SHAPES** | **78** |

Comparison with full scale engineering: use of chucking pieces on components: thin components and use of adhesives: advisability of making fixtures for difficult pieces: three-sided angleplates.

| Chapter Sixteen | **CHUCKS FOR MILLING CUTTERS** | **81** |

Never use taper shank tools or chucks without drawbar: chucks for screwed shank self-tightening collets: Clarkson chuck: Osborn Titanic chuck: Chucks for tee-headed locking cutters: Clare chucks: use of small end mills and D-bits without locking features: philosophy of 'throw-away' cutters.

ABOUT THE AUTHOR   86

INDEX   88

List of Illustrations

Fig.
1	Abwood milling attachment of the 1920s	13
2	E. T. Westbury's milling machine	14
3	Dore-Westbury machine	15
4	Dore-Westbury Mk II machine	16
5	Rodney attachment	17
6	Rodney machine	18
7	Amolco attachment	19
8	Amolco machine	20
9	Mentor machine	21
10	Maximat attachment	23
11	Astra machine	21
12	Twin machine	22
13	Senior machine	26
14	Set of three flycutters	28
15	Flycutting a bracket	28
16	Flycutting connecting rod ends	29
17	Flycutting tapered bar material	29
18	Flycutting cylinder soleplate	30
19	Facemill	31
20	Milling flywheel joint face	31
21	Milling crosshead slide	32
22	Milling bearing jaws in bedplate	33
23	Slitting boss of casting	35
24	Milling feather keyway	37
25	Milling feather keyway on tapered shaft	38
26	Milling keyway with slitting saw	39
27	Set of four Woodruff keyway cutters	39
28	Milling Woodruff keyway	41
29	Fluting locomotive connecting rod	44

30	Drawing of steam hook (lever)	47
31	Photograph of steam hook	48
32	Profiling pad bolt	50
33	Profiling coupling rods	50
34	End-rounding with rotary table	53
35	Cutting teeth in dog clutch part	55
36	Drawing of steady stand for Myford dividing head	56
37	Steady in use on a gear cutting operation	58
38	Throp dividing head	58
39	Thomas versatile dividing head	59
40	Kibbey/M.E.S. dividing head	60
41	Close-up of flycutter and pinion	63
42	Gearcutting with Brown & Sharpe cutter	63
43	Flycutting 10 d.p. gearwheel, front view	64
44	Flycutting 10 d.p. gearwheel, rear view	65
45	Fluting Acme thread tap	66
46	Cutting teeth of ball-end cutter	67
47	Close-up of ball-end cutter	68
48	Gashing flutes in large countersinking tool	69
49	Rear view showing steady stand in use	70
50	Cylindrical machine component being graduated	72
51	Close-up of previous operation	72
52	Graduating part-circular arcuate scale on flat surface	73
53	Tape-held workpiece being flycut	79
54	Hemingway three-sided angleplate	79
55	Two of the three sizes of Hemingway angleplates	80
56	Clare milling chuck	82
57	Clarkson milling chuck	82
58	Osborn milling chuck	83

A Note on the Technical Review

Reviewing this title was interesting. I have been in the industry so long that I would have probably taken a different approach to machining at home, but it is insightful to read and understand that there are people out there with a little bit more creativity than me. This book truly deals with a lot of fundamentals of machining, and, as I usually tell my students, the fundamentals are the same as they were 100 years ago. It is the machines we use that can improve efficiency. This book is set up for home shop environments where efficiency is not an absolute must, so it helpfully references machines that are of the smaller variety and deals with the limits of those pieces of equipment.

—Paul Fiege
CNC Machinist Faculty
Minneapolis Community and Technical College

Preface

In the engineering industry the vertical mill is very widely used, not only for batch production, but also for tool making and the 'one-off' jobs which are so common in general engineering. In the home workshop, where most jobs are 'one-off' the versatility of the machine makes it an important companion to the lathe. This book describes many of the infinitely wide range of operations which can be done, and all those described are illustrated by photographs so that understanding of the methods is assured. These cover work on parts of model locomotives, stationary engines machinery, cutting tools, gears, clutches, etc. Full information is given on the machine accessories which are required, such as various types of cutters and the chucks needed for their mounting on the machine spindle. The use of cheap home-made cutters is shown and encouraged. Guidance is also given on the work-holding devices such as clamps, packings, vises, angle plates, dividing heads, rotary tables, and which of these are needed for particular kinds of work.

CHAPTER 1

Evolution of the Vertical Mill

The horizontal milling machine evolved naturally from the lathe in the first or second decade of the nineteenth century. Eli Whitney (U.S.A.) is said to have had one in use about 1818, and in *Tools for the Job* the late L.T.C. Rolt recounted how the young engineer James Nasmyth (later to become famous as the inventor of the steam hammer and other appliances) fixed one up and milled the flats on hundreds of tiny hexagon nuts for a model of a Maudslay marine engine, while working for Henry Maudslay. Drawings of the early horizontal mills show such a resemblance to the lathes of that period that almost certainly they were in fact lathes which had been adapted to milling. The cutters were really files, made by the file makers of the times, using the 'hand-cutting' methods (really a hammer and a special chisel) which were the only practice available at that time.

The evolution of the vertical mill came naturally after the horizontal machine. I have not found any reliable reference to a date by which the vertical mill had appeared in industry, though this must have been well before 1900.

When model engineering started to become an established hobby at the turn of the century a variety of small lathes

were provided by different makers, and the great versatility of the lathe created in itself a tendency to make the lathe do every operation that arose. This was enhanced by the fact that many modelers were working men with very little cash to spend on their hobby. Many were the ingenious attachments devised to enable the lathe to carry out work it had never been intended to do. Such makers as Drummond Brothers modified their lathes with tee-slotted boring tables to help in this work, and even brought out the famous round-bed lathe, which although intended for a cut-price market, also had built into it the ability to do a lot more than just simple turning. But as the years went by it became ever more apparent something better was needed for milling operations. None of the small mills produced by the machine tool industry were oriented towards the home workshop.

Then in the 1920s the Abwood Tool and Engineering Co. produced an excellent vertical milling attachment for mounting on small lathes, especially the popular $3\frac{1}{2}$ in. flat bed Drummond, though adjustable features made it applicable to other lathes too. It had a No. 1 Morse taper arbor which fitted into the lathe

Fig. 1 Abwood milling attachment of the 1920s

spindle, and bevel gears with keywayed shafts took the drive up to the vertical cutter spindle, which had a No. 1 Morse internal taper. All the gears were equal ratio miter bevels, so the cutter rotated at the same speed as the lathe spindle, and all the six speeds of the lathe were usable. The work was mounted on the lathe boring table, and power feeding in one direction came from the lathe screwcutting gear. A photograph of this unit set up on a Myford Super 7 is shown in Fig. 1. It was unfortunately a low-volume, labor intensive unit with vee slides needing hand scraping, but was selling in 1930 for about $37, about a quarter of the cost of the Drummond lathe. Although out of production for many years now, it was in its time a courageous effort, but belonged to the age when most home lathes were driven by flat belt from a treadle or countershaft, and the cost of electric motors made the independent motor drive uneconomic in home hobby applications.

But the need for a handy vertical milling machine had been recognized, and in the early 1960s that very good friend of model engineers, Edgar T. Westbury, completed an experimental machine, which he described with drawings and photographs in the *Model Engineer* during 1964. That too was a very labor

Fig. 2 E.T. Westbury's milling machine

14 VERTICAL MILLING IN THE HOME WORKSHOP FOR HOME MACHINISTS

Fig. 3 Dore-Westbury machine

intensive machine with vee slides, and the main castings were much too big to be machined in the average home workshop. At that time he was unable to find any engineering firm willing to take it over and manufacture it, or even to do the machining on a contract basis at such a price as it was thought model engineers would be willing to pay.

Three years later I found myself with the opportunity to take a fresh look at this design, which he had discussed with me during the experimental period. I evolved a new set of drawings for a similar machine, but using flat slideways more economically constructed, a reduction gear for lower bottom speeds, hollow spindle for a drawbar, and other changes intended to make economies or improve the performance. This new design was discussed with Edgar, who agreed to the use of the name 'Dore-Westbury', the machine to be sold as a kit of semifinished components by my existing firm Dore Engineering. I was able to place the machining of the components with a number of firms already known to me, and the first sets of materials began to go out to customers early in 1968. Since that time many hundreds of sets have been distributed, all over the world, and are still being made in ever greater quantities by Model Engineering Services, of Chesterfield, who took it over from me in 1971, when I wanted, on account of age, to reduce my commitments.

Castings to the original design are, however, still available from Woking Precision Models of 16 Dovecot Park, Aberdour, Fife, Scotland KY3 0TA, and a machine from these is shown in Fig. 2. The Dore-Westbury machine is depicted in Fig. 3 and the similarity between them will be at once apparent. During its entire life the Dore-Westbury has been undergoing small improvements, and the present suppliers have now decided that the modifications are sufficiently stabilized for the present version to be titled the Mark II model. From now on all machines supplied will be of this form, though still subject to certain optional variations which customers will be able to select as they wish.

The more important changes include an increase in the quill travel from **$2\frac{5}{8}$** in. to **$4\frac{1}{4}$** in. Extra pulley steps with a new type of belt extend the speed range slightly from 32 to 1880 r.p.m. with more intermediates, providing for boring head flycutting on large radii right through to keyway cutting with 1/16 in. cutters. The reduction gear system now fitted has helical gears which run in an oil-bath,

Evolution of the Vertical Mill 15

Fig. 4 The Dore-Westbury Mk II

Fig. 5 Rodney Attachment

Evolution of the Vertical Mill 17

Fig. 6 Rodney machine

sealed against leakage even when inclined away from the vertical, and is quieter than formerly. A larger table, 20 in. by 6 in., can be had as an optional alternative to the normal 16 in. by **5 $\frac{1}{2}$** in. The column and cross tube are steel, as always, but now $\frac{5}{8}$ in. thick and enormously stiff. **2 $\frac{1}{2}$** in. diameter micrometer dials are now standard. The down-feed worm has for convenience been transferred to the right hand side of the head, a coarser pitch rack is now used, and there are a number of other minor improvements.

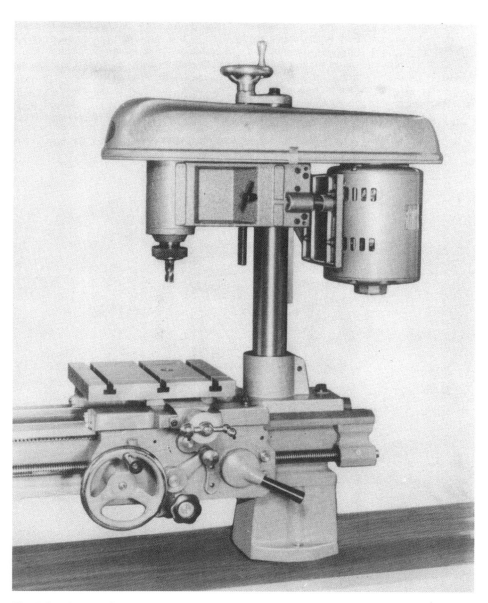

Fig. 7 Amolco attachment

Although colleges and commercial workshops will probably wish to use the all-over belt guard, it may be debatable if the cost of this is justified for the solitary mature modeler alone in his home workshop. An alternative belt guard which covers the spindle pulley only and does not impede belt changing so much is available and is shown on the Mark II machine in Fig. 4.

No doubt the most important improvement is the (optional) provision of power feed for the long movement of the table. A small motor with a 4-step pulley and enclosed worm reduction gear provides feed rates of .5, .62, .85 and 1.1 inches per minute.

A number of attachments similar in general concept, though much different in detail, to the old Abwood, have come on

Fig. 8 Amolco machine

Fig. 9 Mentor machine, now superseded by the FB2 and Maximat attachment

the market in recent years. Tew Machinery produce the 'Rodney' to suit the Myford ML7 and Super 7 lathes, and this is marketed by Myfords. It is shown in Fig. 5 and the complete vertical mill based on this attachment is that shown in Fig. 6.

Another attachment, the 'Amolco' is supplied by N. Mole & Co. Ltd. and appears in Fig. 7. This has its own motor and attaches to the top of the lathe bed also. It is made as a complete machine, shown in Fig. 8.

Fig. 11 Astra machine

Evolution of the Vertical Mill 21

Fig. 12 Twin machine

Elliot machine Equipment supplied a continental machine, the 'Mentor' which was available both in bench and floor mounted forms. The bench machine is shown in Fig. 9. They also have the 'Maximat' attachment to suit the lathe of the same name, which fits on the back of the lathe bed and has independent motor drive (Fig. 10). This is also available as a floor machine, the FB2.

Other complete machines include the 'Astra' supplied by Scot Urquhart, which is really a horizontal mill with an extra vertical spindle with its own motor. Made in several sizes, the small one is shown in Fig. 11.

Twin Engineering Co. introduced a bench machine illustrated in Fig. 12 and also a floor mounted machine of similar size but slightly different design.

Finally the old established firm of Tom Senior Ltd. now produce their type E machine which is floor mounted and shown in Fig. 13.

So it will be seen that there are now many machines and attachments which are of suitable dimensions for inclusion in the limited space of most home workshops. It would be useless to give any details of prices in a book of this kind, as such information would probably be incorrect by the time the book was printed, and readers are therefore recommended to enquire of the various advertisers.

A summary of the leading particulars of all these machines etc. is given in Table 1 but again specifications are amended by makers as time goes by, and it can be no more than a general guide.

A brief word must be said about foreign machines, particularly those coming from Far Eastern countries. It would appear there are several factories producing machine tools and accessories. Some appear to be good, but others are definitely not good, and I do have personal experience of some of these. I have not had the chance to see one of the milling machines working, but those I have inspected in exhibitions have some cheap and nasty features, although the main items such as spindles, bearings, and slideways may be excellent. Some of the machines are more suitable for commercial factories than home workshops but there are others of modest dimensions. To anyone contemplating buying one of these one can only suggest that a close inspection should be made by a knowledgeable engineer, and that a working demonstration should be requested, of the actual machine which is to be bought.

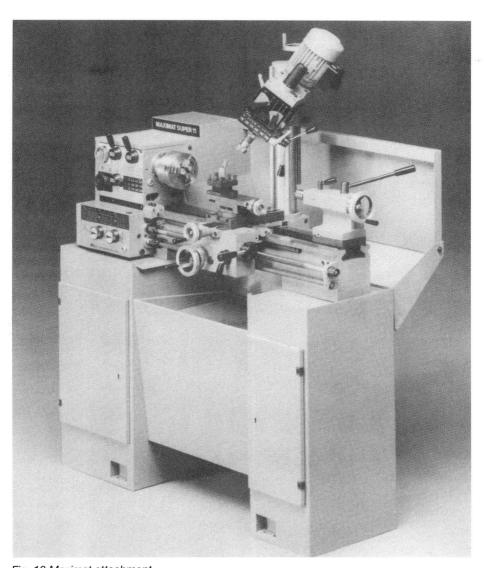

Fig. 10 Maximat attachment

TABLE 1

Make or supplier	Machine or attachment	Table size	Spindle speeds	Spindle nose	Comments
Woking Precision Models Co. Ltd. 1 6 Dovecot Park Aberdour, Fife, Scotland.	'Westbury' bench machine kit of parts.	14 × 6	650, 1120, 1850, 3150	2MT plus Myford thread	Un-machined castings only supplied Head swivels.
Model Engineering Services, 6, Kennet Vale, Brockwell, Chesterfield.	'Dore Westbury' bench machine kit of parts	16 × $5\frac{1}{2}$	**$34\frac{1}{2}$**, 90, 188 304, 790, 1650	2MT plus Myford thread	Now superseded by Mk.II
	Dore Westbury Mk.II bench machine kit of parts.	16 × $5\frac{1}{2}$ (20 × 6 option)	32-1880	2MT plus Myford thread	Complete kit of parts. All machining done that would be difficult in home workshop. Head swivels.
Tew Machinery Ltd. Manor Works Church St. Coggenhoe, Northampton.	'Rodney' attachment.	For Myford ML7 and S77 lathes.	Driven from lathe spindle	2MT plus Myford thread	Rigid head.
	'Rodney plus' floor machine	15 × 4¼	320, 450, 610, 850, 1040, 1490, 2190, 2750	2MT plus Myford thread	Rigid head.
N. Mole & Co. Ltd. 5, Tolpits Lane, Watford, Herts.	'Amolco' attachment.	For Myford & Boxford lathes.	Motor drive. 4 speeds, 325 to 1600	2MT plus Myford thread	Rigid head.
	Bench mill.	15 × 6	325-1600	2MT plus Myford thread	Rigid head.

TABLE 1 (continued)

Make or supplier	Machine or attachment	Table size	Spindle speeds	Spindle nose	Comments
Elliott Machine Equipment, B.E.C. House, Victoria Rd. London, NW10 6NY	'Mentor' machine Bench and floor.	$20\frac{1}{2} \times \frac{7}{8}$	350, 640, 780, 1450	2 MT	Swiveling head.
	FB2 Maximat attachment or floor machine	$24\frac{3}{4} \times 6$	120-2000 (six)	2MT	Swiveling head
Scot Urquhart Ltd., 317, 373a, Earlsfield Rd., Earlsfield, London SW18 3DQ	'Astra' bench and floor machines Hor. with vert, head.	$13 \times 4\frac{1}{8}$	620, 900, 1200, 1850	2MT	Motorized head.
Twin Eng. Co. Caxton Way, Holywell Ind. Est. Watford, Herts.	'Twin' bench machine and floor machine.	20×6	520, 960, 1650, 2880	2MT plus Myford thread	Rigid head.
		20×6	380, 640, 1100, 1900, 3100	2MT plus Myford thread	Swivel head.
Tom Senior, Ltd., Atlas Works, Hightowns Heights, Liversedge, West Yorks.	'Senior type E' floor machine.	$25 \times 4\frac{1}{4}$	480, 950, 1640, 2760	2 MT	Swivel head

Fig. 13 Senior machine

CHAPTER 2

Milling Flat Surfaces

Of all metal-working operations the production of true flat surfaces is perhaps one of the most difficult if reliance has to be placed on hand tools and hand methods, for it depends just about completely on the personal skill of the workman. But a point offset from the spindle center of a vertical milling machine must when rotated describe a flat plane in space if there is no axial movement. Therefore, provided the spindle is truly square to the table, an offset cutting tool must generate a flat surface on a work-piece attached to the table. Model engineering, just the same as full size engineering, demands the production of a great many flat surfaces, so the ability of the machine to perform this task in a simple way, without expensive tooling, is extremely important to the home worker.

FLYCUTTERS

The cheapest tool for the purpose is the flycutter, usually consisting of a small toolbit set in some kind of holder. There are commercially made holders available, but it is easy to make satisfactory holders at home, and they serve just as well. Three home-made flycutters are shown in

Fig. 14. Each is just a Morse taper arbor with an enlarged head having a slanting hole drilled in it to take a cutter bit ($\frac{1}{4}$ in. in these samples) with a screw to lock it in place. The head diameters are $1\frac{1}{4}$ in., **$1\frac{3}{4}$ in.** and **$2\frac{1}{4}$ in.** so the faces that can be machined at one pass are roughly $\frac{1}{4}$ in. to $\frac{1}{2}$ in. wider in each case. They were made by boring through short pieces of steel of these sizes to suit the parallel parts of Morse taper arbors. It is not perhaps widely enough known that tool merchants can, if they will, supply Morse taper arbors of this kind, which are a stock product of the large drill makers. This method of fabricating flycutters by using a ready made arbor with a head Loctited on saves a good deal of time and some heavy steel. The effectiveness of tools made in this way is beyond question. Fig. 15 shows a bracket clamped against a large angle-plate and being milled with one.

Fig. 16 shows one working on a steel connecting rod which has to be reduced from a circular section at each end. The rod is about 9 in. long, so it is held in two vises at the same time, and each end is taken down to finished size before it is turned over. Packings are used, different at each end to ensure the finished surface is above the vise jaws, to avoid cutting

Milling Flat Surfaces 27

Fig. 14 Set of three flycutters

into them, and these packings ensure the rod is at the right attitude for keeping the milled surfaces parallel to the axis.

Owning two vises alike may at first thought seem something of a luxury, but as soon as long articles have to be dealt

Fig. 15 Flycutting a bracket

Fig. 16 Flycutting connecting rod ends

with the benefits are at once apparent.
Another flycutting operation is shown in Fig. 17 where a steel bar is being reduced to a tapered section to cut up into wedge blocks for connecting rods of the type in the previous picture. These wedge

Fig. 17 Flycutting tapered bar material

Milling Flat Surfaces 29

Fig. 18 Flycutting cylinder soleplate

blocks are needed for adjusting the bearings in the rod ends. The rectangular section bar is held in a vise on a tilting angle-plate which has been set at 6 degrees to the table of the mill with a Starrett combination protractor. The tapered form will be seen on the end of the completed piece lying on the angleplate. This is an easy way of getting a special section which cannot be bought, and which would, to say the least, be tedious to make by filing.

These flycutter holders do not allow much adjustment of the radius of the cutter bit, but with some makes of boring head there is a lot of adjustment. For example the Dore boring head permits of using a cutter in a $\frac{5}{8}$ in. diam. bar at any radius up to **2$\frac{1}{2}$** in., and by setting the saddle in or out on the slide body the radius can be adjusted by fine amounts to suit any job within the range. Fig. 18 shows an old type, pre-war boring head being used to face a cylinder sole-plate for a slide valve engine model of 2¼ in. stroke.

FACE MILLS

Of course, multi-cutting-edge face mills permit machining a surface quicker than a single point tool can do, and with less snatch and jerking, but commercially made they are very expensive, and in the home workshop the greater productivity is not usually of much consequence. Nevertheless, for anybody willing to spend the time needed they can be made in the home workshop, with several cutter bits mounted in one mild steel body. Fig. 19 shows a face mill of this kind, which was made originally to screw on the spindle of a Myford lathe to do some repetitive milling of a fairly heavy nature, now no longer required, but it is still a good general purpose tool. It has 12 tool bits $\frac{1}{4}$in. diam. set into flat bottomed holes, all

Fig. 19 Facemill

ground off to the same projection, and sharpened to a diameter of approx. $2\frac{1}{4}$ in.

In Fig. 20 it is shown milling the face of a half-flywheel iron casting for a model stationary engine. The casting is supported by a special angle plate type of fixture, the pattern for which was made in an hour. Without this fixture the operation

Fig. 20 Milling flywheel joint face

Milling Flat Surfaces

Fig. 21 Milling crosshead slide

would be somewhat difficult. If the casting was held in a vise on the table the point of cutting would be a long way from the holding point, and movement of the casting under the pressure of cutting would be not easy to prevent. Vibration and chatter would be more likely. It very often happens that the only way to get a satisfactory job is to make some equipment specially for it. This is not usually wasteful, especially if a duplicate component is ever required, but the equipment is usually found adaptable for some other job later. Doing metal cutting by 'knife-and-fork' methods can soon lead to disaster. The other half of the wheel casting, with the cast-in teeth for the barring 'rack', can be seen in the bottom half of the picture. The wheel is $9\frac{3}{4}$ in. diameter and has 96 teeth.

Broad flat surfaces can be, and sometimes have to be, produced by successive parallel passes with an endmill much narrower than the face required. Apart from taking more time than a tool with a wide sweep, minute ridges tend to be left where the passes overlap, and these may have to be removed later by filing or scraping. So while this method is feasible the flycutter or boring head is better where there is room to use it, and the cutter bits are cheaper than endmills and easily sharpened like any lathe tool.

However, an example of work where a small cutter and successive passes must be used is shown in Fig. 21 where a flat bedplate slide for the crosshead on a model stationary engine is being milled. The surface being cut is in a recess $\frac{1}{8}$ in. deep and the corners cannot be dealt with by a tool cutting the full width, as the radius left would be too great. Note the stop bar bolted to the table. Accurately squared with the table it provides not only correct location for the casting (which was followed by others) but also insurance against slipping.

In the full sized engines these slides were always planed, and every engine-building shop had planers for this kind of work. In the one where I worked there were several of different sizes, and the largest, built by Joshua Buckton of Leeds, could plane any casting up to 20 ft. long, 12 ft. wide and 12 ft. high. It was said at that time to be the largest in Yorkshire, and certainly it often did castings for other firms. Cutting could be done in both directions of the table travel at equal speeds, or in one direction with a quick return the other way. Each of the four toolheads had power operation independent of table movement, so that cross-planing could be done through bearing recesses, etc. One of the pictures shows this operation on a model being done by milling. Each head could also be swiveled so that angular faces could be planed also.

After the planing of crosshead slides they were tackled by the fitters and scraped to a portable surface plate. This was coated sparingly with a mixture of lamp black and oil, slid to and fro on the slide, lifted off, and then all the black marks scraped away. The surface plate was then put on again and a fresh lot of marks made, which in turn were scraped away. This work went on for many hours, indeed on a big slide two men could spend two or three days. For such work the surface plate would be so large that two men could not lift it without the use of the shop crane. Eventually after a long time the finish obtained would be regarded as acceptable. It then consisted of a very large number of extremely shallow depressions between the marks, and each of these proved to be an oil

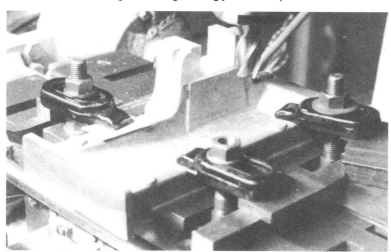

Fig. 22 Milling bearing jaws in bedplate

Milling Flat Surfaces   33

pocket. When the engine was eventually put to work, with the cross-head having had similar treatment, the result was that the cross-head ran to and fro on a film of lubricant which reduced wear to a very small amount. Engines in textile mills would run 60 years and at the end you would find the scraper marks still there. The oil was continuously renewed by brass combs attached to the cross-head which picked up oil from a well at each end of the slide. An engine running night and day, as many of them did, with a speed of about 80 r.p.m. would make approx. 3600 million cross-head strokes in that time! Not a bad performance?

When flat surfaces have to be produced at right angles to the table it is necessary to use the side of an endmill. This may be unavoidable on some components, such as the model engine bedplate shown in Fig. 22. There is not much choice about milling out the jaws for the crankshaft bearings. This is an operation which the big planer used to do with the power drive on the heads of the cross-rail.

CHAPTER 3

Slitting and Cutting

It is common practice to design machinery components with split bosses which can be contracted with a screw for tightening purposes. The slitting can be done with a hacksaw, but if done in unskilful fashion will not look good when completed. Slitting saws and many other disc type cutters can be readily used on the vertical mill by mounting them on a Morse taper arbor having a parallel portion for the cutter, and a nut to secure it. Its a good thing to put a pair of flats on the arbor to hold it by when turning the nut. Fig. 23 shows a slitting saw in use cutting through one side of the boss of one of the parts of the Quorn grinder. On that machine there are several components with this feature, so time will be saved if they are all collected and cut through while the saw and vise are in position.

Fig. 23 Slitting boss of casting

Many other jobs of similar nature will come to mind, such as engine eccentric sheaves, and especially eccentric straps, which can be cast in one piece and then cut through, leaving two surfaces that need only a touch with a file to remove burrs to enable them at once to be bolted together. Not only are castings involved but also parts made from bar material. Marine type connecting rod ends are an example, and this method can also be used for producing bearings in halves.

CHAPTER 4

Keyway Cutting

Keys and keyways are a very common feature of machinery and naturally of models too. The common round-ended keyway, for a 'feather' key, is easily produced on a parallel shaft by holding the shaft in the vise and using a small end-mill, or two-flute 'slot-drill'. Fig. 24 shows the setup for this operation.

Various parts of car and motor cycle engines, gearboxes, and other machinery components in the past have had wheels mounted on tapered shafts with the keyways following the slope of the taper. Modeling one of these would involve following the same procedure. One way in which this can be done is shown in Fig. 25. The vise holding the shaft is set on a tilting angleplate so that the top of the

Fig. 24 Milling feather keyway

Fig. 25 Milling feather keyway on tapered shaft

tapered part comes parallel with the machine table. The shaft shown in the picture is a simple one and short, and could have been just tilted in the vise in a set-up like that of Fig. 24. But a long shaft might well foul the table at its lower end so the elevation which the angleplate gives could in such a case prove essential.

Small endmills are rather frail tools at best and liable to easy breakage. The disc type cutter is more robust and a collection of these acquired either as the need for one crops up, or bought cheaply secondhand, is worth while. Of course the disc cutter cannot always go close to a shoulder on the shaft, and copying a prototype may in some cases rule it out. For the work done in the home workshop there is no need to insist on the relatively expensive side-and-face cutters, (those with teeth on the faces as well as the periphery) because the slitting saw, with teeth only on the periphery, will do well. These are made in a very great variety of thicknesses, and are always coming on the surplus market at low prices. One of these is shown in Fig. 26 milling an ordinary sunken keyway, the shaft being held in a vise with enough overhang to avoid the cutter touching the vise.

WOODRUFF KEYS

The Woodruff key is one widely used in industry. This is in effect a slice off a round bar, cut in half and set into the shaft in a recess made by a small diameter slitting saw. This is rather an oversimplified description, but it will serve well enough as an introduction to the Woodruff key for those in home workshops without industrial experience. Seriously, the Woodruff key, which I think was of American origin, has some very real advantages for the mass production industry, and some of these are of just as great importance in the home workshop and the field of light engineering.

Fig. 26 Milling keyway with slitting saw

For a start the key itself can be parted off from a piece of round mild steel or tool steel. So its diameter is settled with accuracy from the bright bar. The thickness needs careful control, but if it comes off a bit too thick it can be rubbed

Fig. 27 Set of four Woodruff keyway cutters

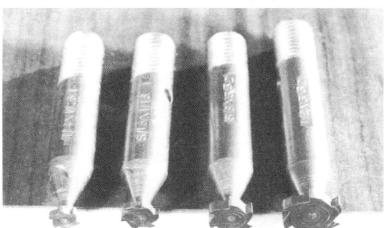

Keyway Cutting 39

down on a flat file. It needs to be cut in two on a line which is nearly a diameter, but the cut edge can readily be filed to bring it to final shape. The keyway is made by a simple cutter like a slitting saw, of the same diameter as the bar from which the key is made, with an integral shank of preferably some standard diameter which can be run true in a collet on the mill. So the shape of the keyway profile – and its width – is settled by the cutter form. The cutting part of the cutter is set in line with

TABLE II

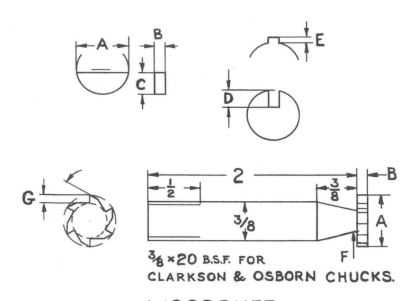

WOODRUFF
KEYS & KEYWAYS   CUTTERS

A	B	C	D	E	F	G
¼	1/16	·109	·073	·037	·100	·030
5/16	1/16	·140	·104	·037	·104	·037
3/8	3/32	·172	·123	·053	·129	·045
½	3/32	·203	·155	·053	·187	·060

the centerline of the shaft, then the cutter is fed in by a predetermined amount.

The resulting keyway is deep enough to give the key a good hold, so that it cannot roll over, and yet the shaft is not unduly weakened. Normally the top of the key is just clear of the keyway in the wheel or lever which is being secured, its purpose being to provide either torque or angular location, and some means such as a set screw may have to be used to prevent endwise movement.

Woodruff cutters are not very cheap, but they can easily be made in the home workshop, from tool steel. The process is really simple. A blank can be turned, making a shank to suit some standard collet, then with the shank held in the collet the working part of the cutter can be turned to its diameter, and thickness. The sides should be very slightly undercut by setting a knifetool a little off square. Using a simple un-geared dividing head the teeth can be cut in two operations using an ordinary end mill; there is no need for angular cutters, as the diagram on the opposite page indicates. The number of teeth is not important, but six is a convenient number for small cutters. It is possible to file the teeth if you do not have access to a dividing head, as the spacing is not at all critical, but it's a little more difficult. Fig. 27 shows a batch of cutters made to the sizes in Table II and Fig. 28 shows a keyway being cut. There seems to be no place where sizes of Woodruff keys and cutters are displayed for model engineers. *Machinery's Handbook* gives sizes which are used in industry, but the sheer range of sizes is itself confusing, and of course the tables are liberally sprinkled with tolerances that modelers could neither follow nor want. I have therefore picked out a few sizes which I think will serve our purpose, and as we don't have to provide interchangeability in our products, if anybody wants to depart a bit from these dimensions he can certainly

Fig. 28 Milling Woodruff keyway

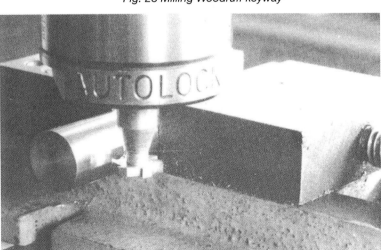

do so. Up to date of writing I have not seen any specification of Woodruff keys in metric sizes.

The cutters shown in Table II have screwed shanks to suit Clarkson and Osborn chucks, which have collets that close on the cutter shank through end thrust exerted by the cutter against the inside of the chuck. If you are making cutters for use in a Clare chuck or just to use in a 3-jaw, these threads are not needed. It may be noticed that the cutters shown in Fig. 27 are stamped with their size details. It is a good plan to have a set of small stamps, say 1/16 in. characters, so that appropriate identity can be marked on all home made tools, jigs, etc as well as model components. The holes drilled in these cutters were provided for the convenience of the hardener. They were hardened for me by a firm where liquid-salt baths are used for heating and quenching tools. A small hole enables the tool to be hung on a wire in the baths without damage to cutting edges.

CHAPTER 5

Fluting Components other than Tools

Fluting of locomotive connecting rods and coupling rods is an operation very similar to keyway cutting so far as the removal of metal is concerned, but the length of the flutes is usually greater, and the length of the pieces demands some well arranged holding methods. One occasionally sees rods which have been fluted with an end-mill by the same method as shown in Fig. 24, giving rounded end flutes like a feather keyway. This is entirely wrong, no full size rods were fluted this way. They have flutes with rounded internal corners in the bottom, and with swept out terminations at the ends, which is done to avoid the notch fatigue cracks which can propagate from sharp corners. Fortunately it is easy to produce flutes which are in accordance with full size practice, and not even necessary to have a fancy milling cutter. A simple tool bit, ground rather like a parting tool, with the corners rounded off, is put into a transverse hole in a cutter bar, and mounted in a chuck on the mill. The rod to be dealt with is fixed edgeways up, as it goes in the loco, preferably against a long angleplate, and the rotating cutter is fed in like a Woodruff cutter would be. When in to proper depth, usually shallow, the table movement is started and the flute is then made progressively along the rod, leaving behind the swept end. Where the cut finishes there is also a swept end, automatically. Coupling rods usually have flutes that are parallel sided, and so do some types of Canadian and American connecting rods. In these cases a single pass with a cutter the right width will complete the job. Most British locomotives, on the other hand, had tapered connecting rods with parallel flanges, i.e. tapered flutes. For these two passes are needed, and this can be achieved in a very simple way.

In Fig. 29 the rod of a Canadian engine is seen fixed on the angleplate. In each end is a screw with a head turned to the size of the hole in the rod end. This is a 12 in. long angleplate with no slots, as holes are drilled and tapped just wherever they are needed for each job. It will be many years before it is so perforated as to be no further use. The two holes for the locating screws are the same distance from the table, and they only provide the location, the rod being secured against the cutting forces by two small clamps as shown. For this rod and for coupling rods the set-up is exactly as shown. But for British type rods, the screw in the big end is made smaller than the hole in the rod by the

Fluting Components other than Tools   43

Fig. 29 Fluting locomotive connecting rod

amount of the taper (at the hole centers) and for the first operation the rod can be allowed to drop down on the screw while the first cut is taken. Then for the second cut the rod is lifted up as far as the screw will let it go, and re-clamped, and a second cut taken. The rod will now finish with a taper flute and two parallel flanges.

This fluting is a very simple operation. The angleplate is extremely rigid. The machine in the picture is happily provided with a $\frac{1}{2}$ in. wide keyway along the center of the table, only $\frac{1}{8}$ in. deep, but a $\frac{1}{2}$ in. square bar can be dropped into it. That enables fixtures to be instantly lined up with the table movement, including dividing heads as well as angleplates. The thrust of the cutter in this example tends to move the angleplate away from the bar, but it is secured with two good bolts in the table slots, not visible in the photograph. It should not be forgotten that locomotive rods which are fluted at all must be done on both sides, but with a set-up like this the job is so simple it would be a pity not to have it right.

CHAPTER 6

Boring

It is not uncommon to have bore holes in components which are much too large to swing around in the lathes that are found in most home workshops. But there is no need in many cases to resort to hand tools, even for holes where great accuracy is not needed. The vertical mill can be used for boring (with a bore tool in a boring head) such things as fire-hole doors in boiler plates, bosses on castings such as long levers, and many other objects. In order to motorize a shaper I had to bore a hole through $\frac{1}{2}$ in. of cast iron to mount a worm reduction gearbox, and this had to be a true round hole. It was done by fixing the casting (15 in. long in one direction from the center of the hole) on the mill table and using a cutter in a boring head. With the worm-actuated down feed, and the bottom speed of the Dore-Westbury machine, **34$\frac{1}{2}$** rpm, an excellent hole was obtained four inches diameter. Without these facilities the work would have been sent out to some engineering firm. The ampler space on the tables of milling machines, compared with what one can get on a lathe saddle with an angleplate, makes the mill invaluable for work of this kind and of course by doing external turning with a boring head one can deal with male registers as well as holes. This is a simple operation too; one just turns the cutting tool inward instead of outward.

CHAPTER 7

Jig-Boring

The term 'jig-boring' is likely to be unfamiliar to many readers of this book, and they may think that whatever it means it must be a long way removed from model engineering. This is not so, for in model making plenty of operations arise that can be done by 'jig-boring' to advantage. Basically it only means fixing a component to the machine table and then using the table screws as measuring devices to position the spindle over any part of the component that is desired before drilling or boring a hole. In many ways this method is better than marking out, measuring with a rule, then center-punching followed by drilling on a drilling machine. For one thing the workpiece is firmly held, the table screws are reasonably good measuring devices, and many holes can be made, of any diameter needed, without losing the attitude of the piece to the table, or one hole to another. Let's take a fairly common component, the beam casting of a model beam engine. This will have several holes to be drilled, usually along one straight line, and rather important, all these should be parallel with one another if the finished engine is to run smoothly. There will be one hole at each end, and a main trunnion hole at the middle, plus one or more for the links of

the parallel motion, pump rods, etc. The casting can be clamped to the table firmly, resting on packaging of reasonable thickness so that a penetrating drill does not dip into the table. At this stage all bosses can be faced with an end mill, even if they are at different levels. The centerline of the casting should have been set parallel with the line of the table movement. Put the drill chuck in the spindle, with a small #2 center drill similar to a center punch, and bring this over the first boss center. Then wind on the table the amount to the next hole and check if the point comes in the right place over that boss. Wind on again to the next and so on checking at each boss. If all come central, all is well. If one or more don't, then an allowance will have to be made as a compromise. Make a note of what it is, re-start at the beginning, and do another run till you are satisfied you have got the right starting point for the best results. If you happen to turn the table screw a bit too far at one of the stopping points, don't worry, but don't turn it back a bit as a correction, because that way you could introduce an error through backlash (lost motion due to slackness) in the screw and nut. Go back to the very start and come at it again. It's a good thing

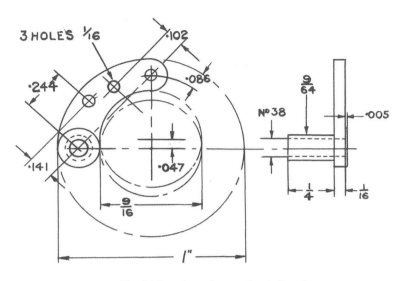

Fig. 30 Drawing of steam hook (lever)

when doing an exercise of this kind to have a paper and pencil handy and write down the micrometer dial readings which are the stopping points. This reduces the chances of accidental error. It is a method used by men in industry who are engaged on delicate work where a momentary interruption can be disastrous. I have myself used it for many years. At this stage drilling can now start. Each hole should be centered with a D-bit ground to about 118 degrees, followed by the appropriate drill, though the larger holes may need a pilot drill putting through first. As each hole is finished, with reaming if needed, move on to the next hole by the table wind, and go through the procedure with that, too. By this method all the holes will be the right distance apart, and will all be parallel to one another in two planes. It will be clear that if any holes are wanted which are not on the main centerline, it is a simple matter to drill these in an off-set position by using the table cross-screw to provide the amount off the main line. When all the holes are finished the beam can be turned over and the bosses milled on the other side.

The beam engine casting is just one example of how this sort of task can be handled. Fig. 30 is a drawing of a component of the trip gear of a model steam engine, and the holes which have to be drilled are in positions which would not be easily attained by the common marking-out and center punching process. Fig. 31 shows one of the finished pieces with one only part-made, to show the method adopted. One inch diameter bar was used, as that gives the outside profile needed. Set true in the four-jaw chuck it was bored 9/16 in., then set out of true by .047 in. and the hole re-bored to the same setting. Next it was set well off center to drill the No. 38 drill hole. The correct setting was established by measurements

Jig-Boring 47

taken off the outside surface of the 1 in. bright bar. With the piece still held, the chuck was removed from the lathe and bolted on the milling machine table. A number 38 drill, running in a true chuck, then 'picked up' the existing hole and the dial readings on both screws of the table were noted (and written down). The drill was changed for a very short stiff 1/16 in. drill, the table screws were rotated, to bring the first 1/16 in. hole position under it and that hole then drilled. Further rotation of the screws brought in turn each of the other holes into position and the drilling was quickly completed. The chuck was then returned to the lathe. The first boss around the No. 38 hole was turned and the piece parted off, care being taken to leave the shallow boss on the parting side. Then the second boss was turned, another parting off, and the two components were through that part of the process. It remained only to cut the desired piece out of the ring and file up the two ends to the rounded profile. By these methods a component of a rather complicated shape was produced under complete control and exactly as specified on the drawing.

There are many other articles in model engineering which lend themselves very well to the jig-boring technique. Locomotive boiler tube plates with a large number of holes can be done this way, and because some of the holes may be $\frac{1}{4}$ in. or even more in diameter it is vital to have the metal clamped down to avoid personal injury, as copper is not one of the kindest of materials for machining. But if clamped on packings on the mill, any large holes for which drills are not available can still be dealt with by using a boring head. If a large drill is available, and the machine has a low enough speed to avoid chatter, there will be no 'three-cornered' holes made to cause embarrassment when fitting flue tubes and silver-soldering them at a later stage. It will be found that as familiarity with the vertical mill develops, other examples will arise in which this high-sounding but really simple technique can be borrowed from industrial practice, with great benefits.

Fig. 31 Photograph of steam hook

CHAPTER 8

Profiling

It is not unusual for large components to have portions which are circular arcs. Locomotive frames are common examples, with cut-aways to clear bogie wheels. Such pieces are much too large to swing in the lathe, and while the band saw if available can do a lot to relieve the tedium of drilling, hacksawing and filing, the mill can do a lot more. Using a boring cutter in a boring head it can take away the unwanted metal in a single operation to finished size on any arc. Alternatively with a boring type tool it can follow the band saw and just avoid the filing.

Smokebox castings for locomotives and traction engines, however, often have circular arcs to fit the boiler shell, and the band saw can be no help with these. But if they are set up on the mill, the radius can be determined by the setting of a boring head cutter, and traverse across the work provided by the downfeed of the spindle, even though this is usually manual. That feed length may not be enough to cover the face width, but after going as far as the spindle will move, a second cut can be taken by resetting the head of the machine.

In machinery details the same problems arise. Fig. 32 shows a pad bolt for locking two machine parts together. The two parts of the pad bolt which are being profiled to suit a round column were made from one piece of steel, and cut apart after the profiling. A groove can be seen where the separating cut was to be taken. The cutter in the boring bar was set to the finished radius. Only the cross-feed of the table was used (to put the cut on bit by bit) the other slide being locked. The tool was traversed by the down feed. It is not possible to take the full amount of metal removal in a single pass in a job like this, but with successive cuts a perfect job is assured. Similarly the holes for such pad bolts are 'part holes' and could not be drilled in the second stage to full size without guide bushes for the drill. But drilling undersize and then opening out with a boring head gets there just the same, a bit less quickly.

Profiling locomotive connecting rods and coupling rods can be a somewhat tiring operation if one has to do it by sawing and filing. Trying to do this work on the boring table of the lathe with vertical slide or angleplate is not very happy either. Usually the cross-slide travel is much too short to complete the length in one pass, so that re-setting is necessary, and the lathe does not have

Profiling   49

Fig. 32 Profiling pad bolt

Fig. 33 Profiling coupling rods

the in-feed facilities needed. Generally with a vertical slide the point at which cutting is being done at the ends of a long rod is a very long way from the place where the slide is secured, so that apart from 'spring' of the piece there is danger of slipping taking place with disastrous results. Compare such attempts with the set-up shown in Fig. 33, where a pair of coupling rods, with 'chucking pieces' of extra metal at each end, are clamped on packings in a safe and rigid set-up. Generally the diameter of end mill used can be arranged to give the right radius where the body of the rod joins the bosses.

CHAPTER 9

End-Rounding

In model work, as in full sized machinery, many components such as crank webs, connecting and coupling rods, machine links, etc. have to have rounded ends. These can be produced by filing, and the use of hardenerd steel collars and rollers for guides has often been recommended in *Model Engineer* to help the not-so-good filer to achieve a good appearance. Even with these, this kind of filing demands a skill which many modelers just do not have (and will never acquire, for want of practice, if nothing else) so for that reason alone it is not a good method. But it is also rather severe on files, which are now expensive tools, and unlikely ever to get cheaper.

So where there is a vertical mill available, why not do the job the right way, as it would be done in commercial engineering? It means investing in a rotary table, but these can be bought in kit form as well as complete ready for use, and if machined and assembled by the home worker himself, are not terribly expensive. Presuming that the component has a round hole at one end, a plug is needed in the table so as to locate by that hole. I have a small rotary table with a $\frac{3}{8}$ Whit. hole in the center and have a number of plugs of standard sizes to fit that.

But another table which I have possesses a No. 2 Morse taper central hole and arbors can be put in this for location. It is, in fact, a Model Engineering Services Type RT3 which does not have a tee-slotted table, but has a spindle screwed like the Myford lathes and will accept any chucks or faceplates from the lathes. This makes it feasible to turn, say, a cylinder cover and transfer it to a rotary table for drilling the bolt holes without losing the accuracy of setting. But that is not a feature of importance for round ending operations. I have used it for a number of engine cranks in the manner shown in Fig. 34. Each crank was located on the arbor but also clamped with a slot plate resting on Picador stepped packings, a pair of these being also under the crank itself. The cutter is a $\frac{1}{4}$ in. end mill cutting on its side.

In all rotary milling of this kind where the cutter is working on the outside of the component it is vitally necessary to feed the table clockwise seen from above. All normal milling cutters rotate the same way as a twist drill, so whichever side of the work the cutter is touching, the work must meet the cutter, and that means clockwise rotation is essential. Otherwise if the cutter is going the same way at the surface as the work it is certain to grab

Fig. 34 End-rounding with rotary table

hold and that means at least ruined work, probably a broken cutter, and a lot of grief. But if one is working on an internal profile, such as trimming the inside of the rim of a flywheel, then the forces are reversed and the work needs rotating anti-clockwise.

Now the threads of the RT3 spindle are like the Myford lathes, right hand, so when one is doing inside work a chuck or faceplate is tightened by the thrust of the cutter. But when doing the, perhaps, more normal milling on the outside of a piece, the cutter thrust tends to undo the faceplate, and unless the work is very light cutting, this is what will certainly happen. The only satisfactory answer to this problem is to drill and tap a hole through the boss of the faceplate, make a coned dimple in the table spindle at the same spot, and insert a screw with a cone point that fits the dimple. Not a difficult matter at all. But if you are going to use a chuck on the same table for the same kind of work, then make a pencil mark to show where the dimple is for the faceplate, and drill the chuck boss well away from this, so that you have two positively separated dimples, each for its own accessory.

I have used a 5/16 in. BSF socket set screw for this purpose, with a point modified (in the lathe) to a longer cone. But I found the ordinary hexagon key was not really long enough to be convenient with a standard 7 ins. Myford faceplate. So I cut off the short bent end of the key and fitted the long part to an extension made of $\frac{1}{2}$ in. bright mild steel. This was drilled in the lathe 3/16 in. deep with a No. 16 drill which is about the across-corners size of the hexagon, then 7/16 in. further with a No. 22 drill which is about the across-flats size. The two pieces were then pressed together in a big vise, the squared-off end of the hexagon cutting its way down the hole in the mild steel. A 5/32 in. cross pin was fitted, Loctited in, and now I have a Tee wrench long enough to reach the screw in the boss without any difficulty. It took only five minutes to make and is a convenience there for ever.

CHAPTER 10

Dividing Heads

For many products the use of a dividing head is an absolute necessity. Many home workers, especially those without any engineering experience, regard them as most mysterious devices, almost bordering on the occult, and say without really thinking, 'Oh. I could never use one of those!'. Well, a dividing head is really no more than a headstock with a spindle on which the work is mounted, with some means of turning it through positive angular amounts, and holding it there when each movement has been made. Naturally there are many types of dividing head and over the years many designs have appeared in *Model Engineer* for heads which can be made in the home workshop. A great deal of satisfactory work can be done with a simple head of the type shown in Fig. 35. On the spindle, provision is made for mounting a lathe change wheel. A spring-loaded plunger with a conical point drops into the gap between two teeth of the wheel, and then the spindle is locked by a screw bearing on a pad inside the main bearing. It is advisable not to rely on the plunger holding the spindle against rotation when screwing on chucks of when fixing a component on an arbor by means of a nut. If the spindle turns, the teeth of the change wheel may be badly damaged. In fact when doing this sort of fixing I always disengage the plunger, then if the screwpad does not hold, no damage is done.

By selecting a suitable change wheel it is possible to get a lot of divisions very easily. For example a 60 tooth wheel will give 2, 3, 4, 5, 6, 10, 12, 15, 20 or 30 divisions. It will not give 8, but a 40 tooth wheel will do so. When doing dividing with this kind of device it is a good thing to have a bit of chalk handy and mark the appropriate tooth gaps where the plunger is going to have to drop in, before starting cutting, to avoid incorrect settings which would ruin the work. Many examples of machinery parts to which a simple head of this kind can be usefully applied could be given. Such items as crankcase drain or filler plugs which need hexagons, square ends on shafts, tools like taps, reamers, parallel flats for spanners on round articles, all these can be formed so very easily with an end mill, with less physical effort than filing, and with an accuracy which enhances the appearance of the article even if dimensional accuracy as such is not important.

But there are examples where accuracy is fairly important, and one which could

54   VERTICAL MILLING IN THE HOME WORKSHOP FOR HOME MACHINISTS

hardly be done at all with hand tools is shown in Fig. 35. This is one half member of a dog clutch. The 12 teeth are being cut with a slitting saw which passes across the work right on the centerline. After each cut, the locking screw was eased, the plunger lifted out, the wheel turned five teeth, and the plunger dropped in again. The spindle was then locked and the next tooth gap cut. Really a very simple procedure. Now on the other half member of the clutch the teeth have to have parallel sides, and the gaps themselves are taper sided. This just involves setting the cutter with its bottom edge above the centerline by half the thickness of the teeth left upstanding in the first half. The same procedure of cutting right across is followed, and after six passes the job is complete. It is feasible, if you are willing to take the trouble, to make a clutch with all tooth sides tapered, so that the two halves are identical. If maximum strength was needed to transmit a lot of power this might have to be done, but it is a good deal more difficult and would rarely be worth the trouble. Unless you are using a well-established design for which drawings are available, it is advisable to lay out the tooth design on the drawing board, preferably at an enlarged scale, to verify the thickness of cutters which will produce the desired result. They may be the same thickness for both halves, but maybe not, it depends on the thickness of tooth selected. It is also a good thing to avoid an odd number of teeth, because the curve of the cutter when going through one side may be chewing into the metal which has to be left intact on the opposite side to make the tooth. If your design can arrange for an even number of teeth this risk will be eliminated. Another point is to check that the desired number of teeth can really be secured with the dividing head you intend to use.

Fig. 35 Cutting teeth in dog clutch part

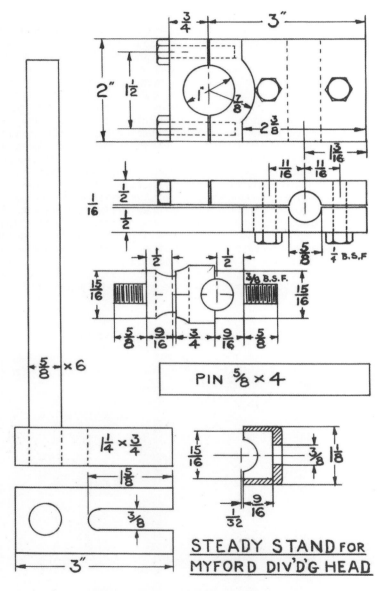

Fig. 36 Drawing of steady stand for Myford dividing head

MYFORD DIVIDING HEAD

The Myford dividing head is an excellent piece of equipment, with a very wide range of divisions. The main spindle has a 60 tooth worm wheel on it, and a single-start worm meshes with that. Concentric with the worm there is provision for mounting a multi-holed division plate which remains stationary and does not rotate with the worm. On the worm spindle is fitted an arm carrying a spring-loaded plunger which has a point of parallel shape that enters holes in the division plate. This arm is slotted and can be set to such a radius as will bring the plunger in the right place for any of the rows of holes that are already drilled in the plate. Having set the arm, if one turns the worm one whole turn and drops the plunger back into the same hole from which it started, the main spindle will have rotated one sixtieth of a turn. But if one moves the worm and arm five complete turns before dropping in, the main spindle will have turned one twelfth of a turn. Basically, that is all there is to getting any desired number of divisions. Having got the right division plate on the head one moves the arm so many turns, plus if necessary, a certain number of holes extra to the complete turns. A chart supplied with the head gives all the available combinations. In order to accomplish all divisions up to 100 it is necessary to have 4 plates, but two of these are needed only for some rather outlandish numbers with which few model engineers will ever have to deal, so the two normal plates will serve almost everything. There is one point of practical importance in using a worm geared dividing head. When moving from one position to the next, always turn the worm the same way, never go back. If by chance you overshoot the right hole, of course you have to turn back, but go well back, way beyond the hole you want by a good margin, then come up to it afresh. If you fail to do this you will have an error in your dividing and a scrapped work-piece. Our old enemy 'back-lash' will see to that. But it's easy enough to avoid this kind of disaster. There is provided on the head a most important aid to correct counting of the number of holes needed when turning the worm. Two brass blades are fitted around the worm shaft, above the division plate, and these can be moved relative to one another, by loosening a screw, and set to embrace the number of holes needed. Than after locking with the screwdriver, they make a mask to show just where the plunger should be dropped in. After each movement you rotate them till one blade comes against the plunger, and you are then ready (after doing the cutting of course) for the next move. In this part of the procedure the two blades move together as if they were one piece of metal.

STEADY STAND

I have found in using the Myford head that it is a convenience to be able to set it at lathe center height when fixed on the boring table. If one wants to drill cylinder covers and similar work the radius of the row of holes can be readily obtained by the cross slide screw and the measurement is direct. So I have a packing block of the right thickness which I can place under it for this purpose.

There is one minor criticism of the Myford head which is nevertheless important from a practical point of view. The single bolt which holds it to a machine

Dividing Heads 57

Fig. 37 Steady in use on a gear cutting operation

Fig. 38 Author's design for simple dividing head

table or vertical slide, etc. does on occasion come a long way from the point where cutting is being done, and accordingly there is danger of the work being ruined by the head slipping. To overcome this I have made up a steady stand from mild steel bar material which bolts on the table of the mill, and clamps on the 1 in. overarm bar of the head. The stand has a vertical $\frac{5}{8}$ in. bar set into a flat base with a slot for a table bolt. A two-way clamp slides on this vertical bar, and another $\frac{5}{8}$ in. bar passes through it horizontally. At the end of this is a two-plate clamp gripping the $\frac{5}{8}$ in. bar, with provision also for gripping the 1 in. bar of the head. The various clamps can be moved separately and make a pretty universal fitting. The whole thing is shown in use in Fig. 37. This fitting of my design is not on the market, but it has proved so useful to me that I am giving a working drawing of it in Fig. 36 and anybody who likes can make a unit for himself.

OTHER DIVIDING HEADS

Since the last edition of this book was printed three new dividing heads have appeared on the market. The first, of my

Fig. 39 The George H. Thomas Versatile Dividing Head

Dividing Heads 59

Fig. 40 The Kibbey dividing head

own design, replaces that shown in Fig. 35, long out of production after the maker died several years ago. It is essentially similar with detail improvements. It has a tailstock for supporting long slender pieces, and a pair of raising blocks which bring the center height up to just over $3\frac{1}{2}$ in. and thereby allow for rotating work up to the size of the 7" diameter Myford faceplate. It is shown in Fig. 38.

The second type is a much more elaborate and versatile appliance designed by Mr Geo. Thomas, and supplied, like the first one, by N.S. & A. Hemingway, 30 Links View, Half Acre, Rochdale. In this head a 24-hole division plate provides for simple dividing with those factors associated with 24. A 40-tooth worm wheel and worm can also be engaged, with a six-row drilled-hole division plate, giving much finer divisions. This plate can be rotated by a subsidiary worm, thereby permitting very high numbers of divisions to be obtained. Most people will need some help to make the fullest use of this device and the book by Geo. Thomas himself on its construction and use, (Dividing and Graduating, Argus Books Ltd.) will be found the best source of information. This head is also available with tailstock and raising blocks, but in normal form is shown in Fig. 39.

The third head is supplied also in kit form by Model Engineering Services, and was designed by Mr Ron Kibbey. It uses standard Myford change wheels as division plates, but has a forked locking plunger which can span over a tooth as well as drop between two teeth. Thus the number of divisions increases to twice the number of teeth in any wheel. In addition it has a mounting for a wheel-pair to mesh with the spindle wheel, giving a gear ratio to add to the basic divisions. It is not at present provided with a tailstock or raising blocks. The head, with extra gear pair in position, is shown in Fig. 40.

CHAPTER 11

Dividing Heads and Gearcutting

The availability of a dividing head is again essential for doing gearcutting on the milling machine. Of course there are types of gears one just cannot do, but ordinary spur gears can be done perfectly well for model engineering purposes, where neither high speeds, extreme silence, nor high rates of power transmission are demanded. The design of gears is a subject outside the scope of this book, which is intended to deal with workshop operations, but there are plenty of sources of information on gear design. The simple type of dividing head already illustrated will serve very well if the gears to be cut have such a number of teeth as the indexing change wheels can deal with. But if the number required cannot be got from existing wheels, then a more complex head such as the Myford, will be needed. Fig. 37 shows this in use cutting the teeth of a pinion which are integral with the shaft. The blank was turned to $\frac{1}{2}$ in. diameter on the part to be held and this was gripped in the standard Myford $\frac{1}{2}$ in. collet, while the other end of the component being centered was supported by a 60 degree center in the overarm fitting. This picture shows the steady bracket described in the last chapter in use. The cutter is a simple flycutter in a boring bar

held for convenience in a boring head. It is shown in close-up in Fig. 41. The profile was established by grinding to suit a wheel of the same pitch with slightly more teeth. The variation is so small as to be of no importance, especially as the pinion rotates at only a low speed.

But if several gears are to be made, and especially if duplicates may be wanted later, it can be worth while to invest in one or more proper disc type gear cutters of what is now universally known as the 'Brown & Sharpe' type, because they were developed by the famous firm of Brown & Sharpe in U.S.A. many years ago. They are of course now made by British firms as well, and by others all over the world, to an accuracy of international standards, far better than anything that is needed for model engineering, and are properly backed off as well as being made from high speed steel. No single cutter will properly deal with all number of teeth, so they are made in sets, each cutter dealing with a limited range, and each bears an identifying number. The range runs as follows:

No. 1 135 to a rack	No. 5 21 to 25
No. 2 55 to 134	No. 6 17 to 20
No. 3 35 to 54	No. 7 14 to 16
No. 4 26 to 34	No. 8 12 and 13

Fig. 41 Close-up of flycutter and pinion

Fig. 42 Gearcutting with Brown & Sharpe cutter

Fig. 43 Flycutting 10 d.p . gearwheel, front view

These cutters can be bought singly at any time from regular tool merchants and I doubt if any discount would be given for buying a complete set of 8. So there is no need to go to the expense of acquiring a complete set unless it is firmly known there will be a use for every one! Fig. 42 shows one of these doing a similar job to that depicted in Fig. 37. The smoother action of the multi-toothed cutter made it possible to dispense with the use of the steady stand, though care was taken not to be too rough with the feed, especially at the start of each cut.

Going now from what might be called the sublime to the ridiculous, or at least from the miniature to the outsize, the next photograph shows the cutting of a much larger gear, actually 9.600 in. p.c.d. This is a gunmetal gear needed as part of a metal pattern from which the flywheel of Fig. 20 was made. It is only 3/16 in. thick but the teeth are 10 d.p., approx. 5/16 in. centers, so a lot of metal had to be removed at each tooth. The cutting was done with a flycutter, ground up by hand to match a silhouette of a 10 d.p. tooth in *Machinery's Handbook,* using a magnifier, this cutter being set in a boring bar of rather excessive length in a boring head. Two cuts were taken, but even then there was a good deal of spring and noise. The shape of the blank casting was arranged to provide for mounting by 8 bolts on the large Myford faceplate, (9 in. diameter) and this was fixed on the mill table so as to overhang the side. That permitted fixing a standard angleplate on the table too, just touching the back of the faceplate, which reduced the springiness of that, and provided a back-stop against the danger of slipping. It would have been asking a lot of the single bolt of the dividing head to prevent movement, under the conditions

Fig. 44 Flycutting 10 d.p. gearwheel, rear view

prevailing, but using this safeguard all went well.

It is well worth keeping in mind in the home workshop that this method of back-up is widely used in the engineering industry, especially in the heavier sections, on planing machines and others where there is either high thrust or high impact, sometimes both, because it can avoid damage to machines and work, as well as possible injury. Fig. 43 shows the front of the gear disc, and in this view the dividing head is not visible. But in Fig. 44 both the angleplate and the dividing head are seen. The gear blank would only just swing in the gap of the Myford lathe so without raising blocks it represents about the largest job that can be turned.

CHAPTER 12

Dividing Heads and Tool Making

There are many occasions in tool making when dividing is necessary. Multiple edged cutting tools like taps, reamers, milling cutters, countersinks, etc. all really need dividing devices to produce the best results, even though some of the simple cutters can well be made by filing or freehand grinding. However, the form of the teeth or flutes sometimes settles that rough and ready methods just will not do, and as in the next example the physical difficulty of getting at the metal that has to be taken away more or less settles that mechanical dividing must be employed. Fig. 45 shows the fluting of a long-thread Acme tap which is held in a collet in the spindle of a simple dividing head, using change wheels for the dividing. In order to

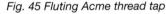

Fig. 45 Fluting Acme thread tap

obtain the maximum chip clearance this tap has five flutes. The head has no tailstock so the outboard end of the tap is rested on a pair of Picador blocks and the clamp rests on another pair. These are very useful accessories for milling operations. Of course each time that a flute is completed the clamp has to be released before the work can be rotated to the position for the next flute. A suitable tailstock, were it available, would obviate the need for this. The 5 flutes are obtained by moving 12 teeth at a time on a 60 tooth wheel. The cutter being used is a commercial tap-fluting cutter picked up cheaply at a sale. These cutters are made with a somewhat lop-sided rounded profile specifically for this duty, but if it had not been available, a flycutter would have been ground up to the profile of a similar tap. The profile is not desperately important and a small error would not matter.

Another example of the use of the dividing head, this time coupled with the use of a small rotary table, is shown in Figs. 46 and 47. The workpiece to be produced was a fine tooth milling cutter with a round end for routing or hand milling on the light alloy cylinder head of a car engine. The commercially available cutters for use in electric drills had such coarse teeth that once they touched the surface of the alloy they were uncontrollable and pulled sideways so violently that damage to the cylinder head was almost a certainty. So as fine pitch cutters appeared to be not purchasable it was decided to make one. The blank, of a carbon steel similar to tool steel but somewhat lower in carbon, was made to hold in a collet and was given a small recess in the end for the fluting cutter to run into. The dividing head, with a 50 tooth change wheel on its spindle, was mounted on a steel plate so that the end

Fig. 46 Cutting teeth of ball-end cutter

Fig. 47 Close-up of ball-end cutter

of the work-piece was beyond the center of the rotary table by half its diameter. In other words, the center of the ball end was over the center of the rotary table. The axis of the work was on the rotation center. This is not apparent from the photograph, but was an essential feature of the set-up. A stop block was clamped to the underside of the milling machine table with a toolmaker's clamp, visible in the photograph, to limit the table movement positively to this position. In the other direction the movement of the table brought the cutter to a part of the tool shank smaller than the diameter at the bottom of the flutes so that indexing could be done with the cutter in the clear. The cutter used was a carbon steel one made originally for producing locomotive lubricator ratchet wheels, with a 60 degree single angle. With the axis of the work parallel to the table a cut was started at the required full depth, and the table traversed along bringing the cutter into operation cutting along the cylindrical portion. When the table was arrested by the temporary stop block, the rotary table was turned by means of its worm, so the dovetail cutter continued cutting round the ball end of the work. When the cutter ran into the recess, the feed was reversed first with the rotary table, then with the main table, back to the starting point, where the cutter was clear of the work shank. The dividing head was then indexed one tooth on the wheel, and a new cut started. Eventually all 50 cuts were completed as shown in Fig. 47.

The working diameter of this tool is ⅝ in. and there are 50 perfect teeth. The tool was hardened and tempered, and when put to use in an electric drill was found to be entirely satisfactory. It worked completely chatter-free, with no tendency to run away, and in spite of its fine and shallow teeth, removed metal at a very

Fig. 48 Gashing flutes in large countersinking tool

gratifying rate. The work on the ports in the alloy head was completed to the great satisfaction of the user, leaving a beautiful smooth surface for the gas flow.

Another example of cutting tool making is shown in Figs. 48 and 49. A large 60 degree countersink was needed for a commercial operation on steel tubes, the tool being about $2\frac{1}{2}$ in. diameter. It was made with an internal form identical with the Myford lathe spindles from a carbon-manganese chrome alloy of known identity, so that subsequent hardening could be done without risk of failure in a commercial establishment with knowledge of this steel. In the picture it is shown mounted on the Myford dividing head having the flutes cut with a special angle form disc type cutter. Because of the peculiar angles which are involved it was necessary to be able to set the head with its axis at an inclination to the table, and it proved that the simplest way to do this was to use a vertical slide. There was a lot of metal to be taken out of the 25 flutes in this decidedly tough steel, and as usual the cutting was a long way from the anchorage point, so the steady stand was brought into use at the back of the head, as it proved too difficult to set it at the same side as the cutter. However, it served well in that position and there was never any suggestion of insecurity.

The main gashes for the flutes were taken out first, with two cuts down each flute. Then the head was tilted to a new angle and another series of cuts taken to accomplish the relief. Because of the conical shape of the work the vertical slide had to have its base set at an angle to the mill table. All these apparently complicated settings had to be established experimentally (though possibly with a lot of effort they might have been calculated) to give the desired form of the cutting

Dividing Heads and Tool Making 69

Fig. 49 Rear view showing steady stand in use

edges of the countersink and the rake angles desired in two directions. The small division plate in use is one which had been made some time previously for doing 125 division micrometer dials, for which unfortunately the standard Myford plates do not provide, or did not at that time. However, with this set-up and not too many hours work it proved possible with home workshop equipment to produce a very suitable special countersink which would inevitably have cost a small fortune if it had had to be made in a commercial factory.

It is hoped that these examples of tool making will encourage all who need non-standard tools, and who know of no firm that would take them on, or are deterred by the high cost of labor-intensive specials. Who knows, somebody in a home workshop might take on the job of helping out some tool factory that would not want to be diverted from its normal work by jobs of this kind?

CHAPTER 13

Dividing Heads and Graduated Scales

In the construction of small machine tools and accessories it is often desirable to have graduated scales for the convenience of precise measurements, and the cylindrical micrometer dial is undoubtedly the commonest type. Depending on the number of graduations required the engraving or cutting of the lines can be done with either a simple head or the worm geared type. There is a choice between using a non-rotating cutter of the planing or slotting type, and using a rotating cutter like those employed on pantograph engraving machines. In each case the work is mounted on the dividing head and the table screw is used to move the work against the tool. It is advisable to clamp stops to the table, if the machine does not have stop devices built in, so as to positively limit the table movement and keep the lines the correct length. Where there are lines of more than one length on the same dial, one or more slips of sheet metal can be inserted in front of the stop to obtain the short lines. The cutting tool can be ground to an included angle of about 50 degrees. Few modelers have access to an engraving cutter grinder, which is the ideal machine for grinding the D-bit type cutters with conical end which are needed, but they can in fact be ground on the Quorn grinder, which is becoming more and more popular with model engineers. Those who do not possess one of these versatile machines may have some friend who can help out by grinding an occasional cutter. For my part I prefer the rotating cutter but then I do have the machine to grind them. Without this a slotting tool can easily be ground and if rigidly held will also do a good job.

Fig. 50 shows a cylindrical scale being engraved on the mill with a rotating tool. This is not a loose collar, the scale is on the component itself, actually part of a Quorn grinder, but a separate collar would just be mounted on an arbor and treated in the same way. Fig. 51 is a close-up of this operation.

Some articles need the scale on a flat surface but still in a curve. One of these is needed on the Quorn grinder, and Fig. 52 shows this set on a rotary table on the mill and being dealt with by a rotating cutter as the last example. The M.E.S. table in the picture has a 90 tooth worm wheel, so one revolution of the worm gives 4 degrees movement and each division on its 16-line micrometer collar gives one quarter of one degree. The scale being engraved is one specified in degrees, as it is an angle-setting scale.

Dividing Heads and Graduated Scales 71

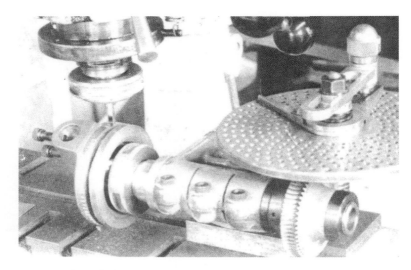

Fig. 50 Cylindrical machine component being graduated

Fig. 51 Close-up of previous operation

Fig. 52 Graduating part-circular arcuate scale on flat surface

Conical micrometer collars are sometimes required, but they are more difficult to produce and should be avoided in the designing if at all possible. For graduating one of these the dividing head would need to be tilted after the fashion of that in Fig. 48, but possibly in the other direction, depending on the actual design of the collar.

One point in making scales of any kind. The figuring should always be done so that the figures are the right way up as seen in using the scale. The figures may need to have rising value . . . 10, 20, 30 . . . to the right hand from the zero mark, but possibly, depending on circumstances they may need to be the opposite way. It is as well to get this thoroughly sorted out before starting to use marking punches to put the figures in, because it can be very difficult to retrieve the situation if the start was made the wrong way.

CHAPTER 14

Cutter Speeds for Vertical Milling

In general I am afraid model engineers do not have very clear ideas about how fast they should run their lathes, drills or milling machines. To run too slowly extends the working time unnecessarily, but to run too fast will soon dull a cutter and may also cause poor work finish through chatter. The wear on milling cutters (apart from flycutters) is important because of the trouble of sharpening them, and broken cutters can be an expense. The principles which govern the speeds of cutting metal in other machines such as the lathe and drill can be taken as a useful guide, in the sense that any speed which an a particular material will dull a lathe tool or drill will likewise dull a milling cutter. But on the vertical mill there are other problems too. Generally the point of cutting is much further from the support than that of the lathe tool. It will also be a long way comparatively from the spindle bearings. The work may be much further from the slideways than it would be from the bed of the lathe. The cutting tool is normally unsupported at its cutting end, and its own elasticity is added to that of the chuck, spindle, work, etc. So speeds which might be feasible on the lathe may well be found much too high on the mill.

As an example, turning back to Fig. 20 will show how elevated the surface of the work is from the table slides, and in this example low speeds were essential to obtain a reasonably good finish.

The rates of feed and depth of cut which are commonplace on industrial machines are out of order in the home workshop. Not only are industrial machines heavy and rigid, so are the work holding devices, and the work itself is much more robust and rigid. Also, and this applies particularly when cutting steel, these machines can usually flood the cutter with coolant, taking away the heat generated in the cutting operation, and that is not normally possible on machines in the home workshop. So Table III has been compiled to give some guidance in the kind of operations which have been described in the book. It is based on using speeds which will conserve the sharpness of the cutters likely to be used. For flycutters, commercially made endmills, and Brown and Sharpe gear cutters, the tools themselves will be properly hardened high speed steel. For the Woodruff cutters it is based on these being home made cutters produced from carbon steel or tool steel (which is a carbon steel with about 1.2% carbon and no alloy). More than one article in *Model Engineer* in years past has described methods for making gear cutters of the Brown and Sharpe type, and I have some of these myself, made from plain carbon steel of about 1% carbon. Such cutters must be run more slowly than the high speed steel cutters of commercial make, but it is possible that a wider variety of tools will in future be made in the home workshops, as a better understanding of tool making and the contribution which the vertical mill can provide comes to be recognized. The cutting speeds to be used with such tools will need to be arranged to suit the tool materials and the work they are doing.

The proper mounting of tools in the mill is a matter of great importance. Reference has already been made to tools which screw directly on the spindle nose, and another chapter in this book will give descriptions of the milling chucks which are currently available.

It will be found that some of the mills at present on offer have speed ranges which do not go low enough to match the bottom end of the recommended speeds on Table III. This is unfortunate, but it is a fact of life, and one must do the best one can with it, even it it means occasionally borrowing the use of a friend's machine. Naturally it will tend to influence the decision when thinking of purchasing a machine.

TABLE III

FLYCUTTING. Flat surfaces as in Fig. 1 6, H.S.S. cutters, easily sharpened.
Depth of cut:

Mild steel	.030 in.
Brass	.045 in.
Light Alloy	.060 in.

(inches)

Diameter of cutting:	1	$1\frac{1}{2}$	2	$2\frac{1}{2}$	3	$3\frac{1}{2}$	4	$4\frac{1}{2}$	5
Speeds r.p.m.:									
Mild Steel	150	100	75	60	50	45	38	34	30
Brass	230	150	115	90	75	65	57	50	46
Light alloy	570	380	285	230	190	165	145	125	115

Speeds may well be limited by the extent that chip thrown about the workshop can be accepted.

ENDMILLING. Spiral flute H.S.S. endmills. Depth of cut up to $\frac{1}{8}$ of cutter diameter up to 3/16 in., then up to $\frac{1}{4}$ of diameter. Width of step being cut up to $\frac{1}{4}$ of diameter.

(inches)

Cutter diameter	1/16	3/32	1/8	3/16	1/14	3/8	1/2	5/8	3/4
Speeds r.p.m.:									
Mild steel	1800	1500	1200	800	650	450	350	250	180
Brass	2500	2000	1600	1150	850	650	450	350	250
Light alloy	3500	3000	2500	1700	1400	1200	900	800	700

KEYWAY CUTTING. H.S.S. spiral fluted endmills or slot drills. Fig. 24.

(inches)

Width of keyway	1/16	3/32	1/8	3/16	1/4	3/8	1/2	5/8	3/4
Depth of cut:	(thousandths of an inch)								
Mild steel	10	15	25	30	45	70	100	200	250
Brass	12	17	27	40	60	100	140	250	300
Light alloy	15	18	30	45	65	110	135	300	350
Speeds r.p.m.:									
Mild steel	1800	1500	1200	800	650	450	350	250	180
Brass	2500	2000	1600	1150	850	650	450	350	250
Light alloy	3500	3000	2500	1700	1400	1200	900	800	700

TABLE III (continued)

KEYWAY CUTTING. With H.S.S. disc cutter Fig. 26, or slitting Fig. 23.

			(inches)		
Cutter diameter.	2	$2\frac{1}{2}$	3	$3\frac{1}{2}$	4
Speeds r.p.m.					
Mild steel	65	55	45	38	33
Brass	115	95	75	65	55
Light Alloy	190	155	125	110	95

GEARCUTTING. Commercial H.S.S. Brown & Sharpe cutters $2\frac{3}{8}$ in. diameter. Fig. 42.
Speeds r.p.m.

Mild steel	48
Brass	80
Light Alloy	110

'Home-made' cutters produced from 'tool steel'.

	(inches)			
Cutter diameter.	$1\frac{1}{4}$	$1\frac{1}{2}$	2	$2\frac{1}{2}$
Speeds r.p.m.:				
Mild steel	60	50	38	30
Brass	120	100	75	60
Light Alloy	180	150	110	90

WOODRUFF KEYWAYS. Using 'home-made' tool steel cutters. Speeds may be increased by one third for commercial H.S.S. cutters.

	(inches)			
Cutter diameter.	1/4	5/16	3/8	1/2
Speeds r.p.m.:				
Mild steel	380	300	250	200
Brass	700	580	450	350
Light Alloy	1000	900	800	650

Cast iron, unless exceptionally hard, may be cut at the same revs. as mild steel, but for work on carbon steel ('tool steel'), alloy steels, and free cutting stainless reduce revs. by one third. For non-magnetic stainless reduce by half.

CHAPTER 15

Work-holding with Difficult Shapes

Problems do arise from time to time regarding the methods of holding work in the milling machine. In full scale engineering these problems are not nearly so acute as components are more solid and clamps can be applied without crushing the pieces. Often with model parts it is difficult to get a hold sufficiently firmly without more or less mutilating the piece. One method I often use both for castings and bar material is to arrange for an accurate chucking piece to be left on the component until all operations are complete and then to remove this. Generally this piece is made to suit one of the Myford collets, from $\frac{1}{2}$ in. diameter downwards, since the collets do hold the part with great accuracy, and after turning operations it can be transferred to the mill with the collet placed in a dividing head; even if no indexing has to be done, the head acts as a very effective vise.

Sometimes thin components present problems in holding on the milling machine. If one side is already flat one can use double-sided sticky tape, available from drawing office supply shops and some stationers. If two or three strips can be used, an astonishingly firm grip can be obtained, which will stand up to shear forces induced by milling. I have also in an industrial plant stuck down metal which had to be tooled all the way across the piece, on a false base with woodworker's glue and a sheet of newspaper. After the operations are completed a fine chisel is knocked in between the parts and the paper tears within its thickness, so the pieces come apart with some paper sticking to each. This can then be washed off with hot water. There is nothing very original about this, of course, it is an age-old patternmakers' method of producing a pattern which has eventually to be in halves, but it is a sound method not nearly so well known as it should be. Fig. 53 shows a light alloy casting being faced right across with a flycutter, the casting being stuck to the table with sticky tape and nothing else.

However, the various examples given throughout the book should serve to show how to undertake a really wide range of jobs. At the risk of seeming repetitive I would again stress that it is often worth while to make a jig for holding or locating the work, just to make sure it can be held firmly enough without damage in the right attitude. The kind of jigs and fixtures needed in modeling seldom involve more than a few minutes or perhaps an hour to make, and if this safeguards the compo-

Fig. 53 Tape-held workpiece being flycut

Fig. 54 Three-face angleplate used to align vee-blocks

Work-holding with Difficult Shapes   79

Fig. 55 Three-face angleplates used as main packing

nent, as well as the tools and machine, it is time well spent. If a duplicate component is ever needed that will be produced expeditiously without risk too.

Angleplates

A new type of angleplate has been introduced by Hemingway. This has three faces machined at 90 degrees to one another. I have found over many years that cast-in slots in angleplates never seem to be in the right place for any job, and it seems better to just drill a hole where it happens to be needed. These angleplates, which are sent out unmachined in light alloy, are in three sizes very convenient for use in home workshops and can easily be faced up on the Myford lathe boring table or faceplate. Fig. 54 shows one of them set across a mill table to locate the two vee-blocks in which the work is resting. Fig. 55 shows another pair used as main packings with Picador stepped blocks on top to give the last bit of height adjustment for the clamp plates. So many sizes are available by selecting different attitudes of these blocks that they are very useful indeed.

CHAPTER 16

Milling Chucks for Safe Cutter Holding

The newcomer to vertical milling may wonder why there should be any need for special chucks for milling cutters, and especially when he sees that these are fairly expensive accessories, may be tempted to make do without one. But first of all it is necessary to realize that the forces acting upon milling cutters in use are generally different from those acting on drills in a drilling machine or lathe. The drill is usually subjected, except at the moment of complete penetration, to axial forces only, which press it more and more firmly into the Morse taper hole in the spindle. Even if it is held in a drill chuck and has a parallel shank, the same thing applies.

But the milling cutter is subjected to transverse forces, across the axis, and unless it is screwed on the spindle, these forces have a component which is pressing against the inside of the Morse taper hole, and thereby trying to cause the cutter to slide out of the spindle. Each time the spindle rotates the pressure is transferred to the opposite side of the hole, and this waggles the tool out of the spindle. So first of all, any tool mounted by a taper shank, whether it is a chuck or a solid endmill with taper shank, MUST be provided with a drawbar through the spindle to stop this tendency to work out.

For cutting tools which in operation produce no end forces that precaution is sufficient. But all the spiral fluted endmills and slot drills do generate end forces, tending to screw them out of the holding device. (Strictly speaking this applies to cutters with right hand rotation, like a drill, and right hand fluting, also like a drill. But as it would be remarkable for any others, though manufactured, to be found in a home workshop, the others can well be disregarded.) So spiral fluted cutters will try to work out of a chuck, if parallel shanked, and must be forcibly prevented. It is not good enough to hold them in a three-jaw lathe chuck, especially since most of these exert more pressure at the inner end than the outer, through wear existing in the jaw slides, in effect giving them a slight taper.

This is where the specially designed milling chuck comes into its own. There are two basic types, but each is arranged to grip the cutter firmly on its parallel shank by a split collet closed by a screw thread forcing the collet into a conical part of the chuck. In addition one type uses cutters formed with a special shaped end,

Milling Chucks for Safe Cutter Holding　81

Fig. 56 Clare milling chuck

and the other type uses cutters with a short screw thread at the end of the shank. The first of these, the Clare, has a rectangular end for the cutter, and this end is undercut by milling. After passing it through a rectangular slot in the collet, the cutter is turned through a small angle, so the part not undercut overhangs the end of the collet, and cannot slide out.

The collet is not only retained in the chuck body by an internally screwed cap which fits on the body, but is also closed on the shank by it. The collet screws into another thread in the cap, which ensures that it loosens when required, a small spanner being provided by the makers for this purpose. This type of chuck will in fact hold cutters which do not have the 'tee'

Fig. 57 Clarkson milling chuck

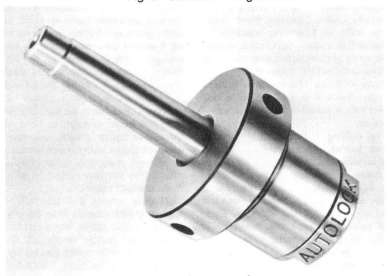

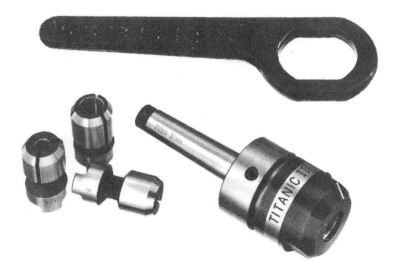

Fig. 58 Osborn milling chuck

end, and have just a plain round shank, though of course the security feature is then non-existent. But for small cutters and light duty it will serve very well.

The other type of chuck, made both by Clarkson and Osborn, uses only a screwed shank type of cutter and cannot be used except with this. The screw thread on the shank, when subjected to the torque necessary to drive the cutter, provides the force to close the collet and thereby grip the tool shank. A center device inside the body engages with the center dimple in the end of the cutter to reduce friction forces that would hamper rotation of the cutter. The Clarkson chuck needs a spanner, provided with the tool, to release the collet for changing cutters. The Osborne uses a finer thread on the securing sleeve, together with some lost motion provisions, and can be released by hand without the use of a spanner. There is provision with each of these for using 'throw-away' cutters, which are made cheaply in sizes up to $\frac{1}{4}$ in. These have a plain shank, unscrewed, of $\frac{1}{4}$ in. diameter whatever the size of the cutting portion, which has a small flat in one place. They are set in an adapter with a small screw at the side, which bears on the flat, and this is sufficient to prevent their working out of the chuck. The idea of these cutters is that they are made so cheaply that in a commercial engineering shop it will cost more to re-sharpen one than to replace it by a new one. Whether or not that is really true will depend on the particular establishment in which they are being used, but in the home workshop, if there is a Quorn grinder, it will be feasible to re-sharpen them at a worthwhile cost in time and trouble, for a while, until a certain amount

Milling Chucks for Safe Cutter Holding   83

of shortening has taken place.

All the cutters with screwed ends to suit the Clarkson and Osborn chucks have Whitworth form threads 20 per inch irrespective of diameter. On $\frac{1}{4}$ in. shanks this conforms to B.S.W. and on $\frac{3}{8}$ in. shanks to B.S.F. for both of which dies can be readily obtained. But for other diameters, if one needs to make a special cutter in the home workshop, screwing a shank 20 threads per inch is not a difficult task. Making the special ends for the Clare cutters is not so easy in my view, but the Clare chuck has the advantages of a short overhang and a smaller diameter of body. This is particularly useful when holding work in a 3 or 4-jaw chuck on a dividing head, when sometimes it is difficult to clear the chuck jaws. But all these chucks can be fully recommended as being good precision tools which provide complete security against cutters working out in use. If an accident of that kind happens due to not having a security chuck, a ruined component is certain, a broken cutter is possible, and I have seen this happen on a number of occasions. So do be warned, and don't think the cost of a proper chuck is too high to face.

Photographs of the three chucks mentioned are shown in Figs. 56, 57 and 58. The Clarkson Autolock chuck shown here, as well as in pictures in the text, is fitted with a damping ring. After the chuck is fixed in the Morse taper, this ring can be screwed up to contact the end of the machine spindle, giving extra support against vibration.

ARNOLD THROP was an apprentice then an Outside Erector with the famous engineers Cole, Marchent & Morley, Bradford, Yorks. Products: compound engines to 2500 hp, Uniflows to 1500 hp, Diesel oil engines, condensers for largest power stations. Later he held technical-administrative posts in high-tension switchgear, mining machinery, stainless fabrication, machine tools, and marking devices. At his retirement he was the Director of Engineering, Edward Pryor & Son, Sheffield.

He has been an I.Mech.E. in mounting seniority over 50 years, serving on several committees and one of B.S.I. He has read papers to I.Mech.E. and the Newcomen Society of which he is a member. He has worked for half a dozen years as demonstrator on the Workshop Stand of S.M.E.E. at Model Engineer Exhibitions, contributed articles to *Model Engineer* from 1932, and having been in Sheffield S.M.E.E. from 1937 has been its President for some years.

Founding Dore Engineering in 1963, he redesigned Edgar Westbury's vertical mill and sold it as the Dore-Westbury until transfer to Model Engineering Services in 1971.

His present interests are stationary engines, workshop equipment, gardening and photography.

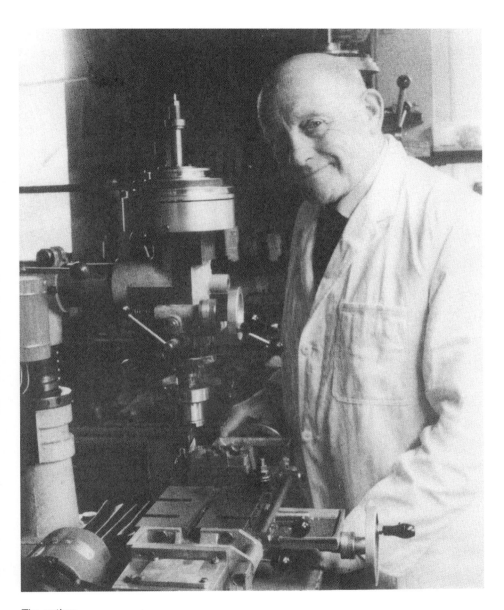

The author

Milling Chucks for Safe Cutter Holding 87

Index

Abwood milling attachment	12
Amolco milling attachment and machine	21
Angleplates	80
Angleplate used as backstop	27, 29
Arbors for slitting saws and disc cutters	35
Astra milling machine	22
Boring operations	45
Boring heads	30
Chucks, Clare, Clarkson, Osborn	82
Clutch teeth	55
Connecting rods	43
Crosshead slides, engine bedplate	32
Dividing heads, description and principle	54
Plain type, change wheel indexing	55
Myford worm-geared type	57
Use of division plates	57
Use of locating blades	57
Packing block for center height	57
Steady stand for extra rigidity	56
Dividing heads and gear-cutting	62
Plain type	62
Pinion cutting	62
Large gear cutting	64

Dividing heads and graduated scales	71
Planing/slotting and rotating tools	71
Table stops and line length control	71
Cutting/engraving cylindrical scale	72
Cutting/engraving flat arcuate scale	73
Conical micrometer dials	73
Marking figures of scales right way	73
Dividing heads and tool-making	66
Fluting screwing tap	66
Cutting fine tooth milling cutter	67
Cutting large countersink	69
Special division plate, 25 hole	70
D-bit for hole centring to start drills	47
Dore-Westbury milling machine	14
End-rounding:	
Filing collars and rollers	52
Using rotary table	52
Fittings for rotary table	52
Rounding engine cranks	52
Direction of table rotation	52
Locking precautions for external work	53
Engine bedplate bearing jaws	33
Engine cylinder soleplate	30
Evolution of vertical mill	12

Fluting operations, locomotive rods, correct flute form	44
Rods for British engines	43
Rods for Canadian and American engines	43
Flywheel (in halves) joint face	31
Gear cutting	62
Grinder for engraving cutters and D-bits	71
Identification of cutters etc. by marking when made	42
Jig-boring:	
Measuring by table screws	46
Written record of measurements	47
Example of beam for model engine	47
Trip gear lever of model engine	48
Boiler tube plates	48
Avoidance of back-lash errors	46
Jigs for milling operations	78
Keyways for plain sunk keys:	
Endmilling feather keyways on plain shafts	37
Keyways on taper shafts with tilting angleplate	38
Disc cutter milling of keyways	41

Loctiting for permanent assembly	27
Long components, holding problems	38, 49
Machine specifications, table of	24
Maximat milling attachment	22
Mentor milling machine	22
Milling cutters, multi-tooth:	
Early (19th century) 'file-cut' cutters	12
Facemills	30
Endmills	38
Slitting saws	35
Disc cutters	40
Woodruff cutters	40
Brown & Sharpe cutters	62
Tap fluting cutters	67
Angle cutters	69
Milling cutters, single tooth:	
Flycutters	27
Connecting rod fluting cutter	43
Profiled gear tooth cutters	62
Engraving cutters	71
Milling operations:	
Flat surfaces parallel	
to table	32
Flat surfaces square	
to table	34
Slitting and cutting	35
Component fluting	43
Tool fluting	67
End rounding	52

Gear-cutting	62
Keywaying	39
Woodruff keys and keyways	38
Boring	45
Jig-boring	46
Profiling	49
Engraving	71
Myford-Rodney milling attachment and machine	21
Myford collets	62
Myford dividing head	57

Profiling:

Circular arcs	49
Locomotive frames	49
Smokebox and cylinder saddles	49
Pad-bolts	49
Small arcs derived from curve of endmills	51

Quorn grinder for tool sharpening	83
Quorn grinder, parts of	35, 71

Rotary tables	52
Rotary table, M.E.S.	52

Senior milling machine	22
Security of milling cutters:	
Forces acting upon drills and cutters	81
Use of drawbars in machine spindles	81
Positive locking of screwed cutters in chucks	82
Positive locking of Tee cutters in chucks	82
Slitting and cutting operations	35
Speeds of milling cutters	74
Tapered sections	29
'Throw-away' cutters	83
Twin milling machine	22
Vises, use of two together	27
Westbury, Edgar T.	14
Westbury milling machine	14
Woodruff keys and keyways	38
Work holding for difficult shapes:	
Use of chucking pieces later discarded	78
Sticky tape for thin articles	78
Glue and paper for thin articles	78
Specially made jigs for difficult shapes	78